I0164005

Follow Me

To include:

Feel Deeply
Faith, Hope *and* Love
Freedom

Neville Goddard

MB

Copyright © 2018 Merchant Books

ISBN 978-1-60386-768-9

DIGITALIZED BY
WATCHMAKER PUBLISHING
ALL RIGHTS RESERVED

Contents

Follow Me

We are told that when Jesus found Philip, he said: "Follow me." Then Philip told Nathanael: "We have found him of whom Moses and the law and the prophets wrote." Philip is one who is interested in the workings of the mind. Looking for one who is searching for the source of the phenomena of life, Jesus finds one in whom he can reveal himself.

The Book of John begins: "In the beginning was the Word and the Word was with God and the Word was God." Now turning into a person, it is said: "He was in the beginning with God. All things were made through him and without him was not anything made that was made. In him was life, and the life was the consciousness of men."

Read this statement carefully and not superficially, and you will discover that from the beginning-less beginning there has been God, and another through whom God acts and by whom God expresses himself. One who is to God what man's imagination is to a man. They are inseparable, for the Word is not only with God, but is God!

Man finds it difficult to identify himself with his imagination, but the word "logos" – translated "Word" means a purpose; a plan; a pattern. The Word which was with God in the beginning is Divine Imagination, through which all things are made. There is not one thing in the world today which was not first imagined. Perhaps you cannot grasp the idea that nature was first imagined, but you cannot deny that man's clothing, home, business, and transportation, were imagined.

Man expresses himself through his human imagination, just as God expresses himself through his Divine Imagination. There is no clear-cut separation between God and Imagination, or man and his imagination. I tell you, Imagination is God Himself. He is the divine body Jesus, of which we are his members. Identifying Divine Imagination with Jesus, Blake claims Imagination became Man, that Man may become God's power and wisdom, called Christ. Any Christ other than he who is crucified, buried, and rises in an individual is false, for there is no Christ other than man's own wonderful human imagination.

God's creative power is buried in you. Just as a seed buried in the womb of woman must bring forth after its own kind, God's power is brought forth as your spiritual birth. Your imagination is spirit buried in you. God – being spirit – has planted his seed, which will erupt one day, and you will experience a spiritual birth.

In the 3rd chapter of the Gospel of John, he speaks to one who is a member of the Sanhedrin, saying: "Unless a man is born from above he cannot enter the kingdom of heaven." Why? Because it is impossible to physically enter that which is spirit. The kingdom of heaven, being spirit, can only be entered through a spiritual experience. Nicodemus, accepting this statement on a physical level, asked: "How can a man who is old re-enter his mother's womb and be born again?" His question was answered in this strange way: "The wind blows where it will and you hear the sound thereof, but you cannot tell from whence it comes or whither it goes. So, it is with everyone who is born of the spirit. (wind)."

When I was born from above I was aware of a peculiar, unearthly wind. This wind is a must in order for man to leave this sphere of death and enter the eternal sphere of life called the kingdom of heaven.

One cannot speculate upon God's kingdom by using images of earth for, "Eyes have not seen or ears heard what God has prepared for those who love him." If your eyes have not seen or your ears heard of that age, don't try to speculate using images of earth, for there is nothing here that remotely resembles the kingdom.

Now let me share my experiences with you. I retired one night, never suspecting that the time of delivery was upon me. I had been carrying God's plan of salvation within me since the beginning of time. It had been growing, yet I did not suspect its birth.

That night as I slept, I felt an unearthly vibration possess me. It increased in intensity until I felt I must explode, when suddenly I began to awake. Expecting to see the room I had fallen asleep in and the normal awareness I have known after a dream of the night, I awoke to a greater awareness – to discover I was in my skull, which was a tomb in which I was buried.

Alone, I arose to discover my skull was sealed and there was no escape. I knew I had awakened in my head, yet all of the outlets through the eyes, ears, and mouth were sealed. Intuitively I knew that if I pushed the base of my skull I would be set free. I did and as something moved I squeezed myself through that little opening, just as a child comes out of the womb of a woman. When I was completely free, I looked back at the head from which I had come. It was ghastly pale, turning from side to side as though recovering from a great ordeal.

I had no idea I had been sleeping in that head, but thought it was my very being. It had never occurred to me that the spirit which gave me life was the cause of my breathing and consciousness. I thought my physical body was me, not realizing it was simply where the real me was buried.

Once out of my skull, an unearthly wind caused my head – as well as the house – to rattle. Looking for the cause, my attention was diverted for a few seconds. And when I looked back, my body was gone and in its place were my three brothers. One was sitting where the head had been, while the other two were sitting at the feet. Disturbed by the sound, one rose and moved in the direction of the wind. Looking down, he said: "Why, it's Neville's baby." The other two questioned his words, saying: "How can Neville have a baby?" Without arguing the point, my brother reached down, picked up a baby wrapped in swaddling clothes, and placed it on the bed. Then I, as though having rehearsed the drama in eternity, took the babe in my arms and said: "How is my sweetheart?" as the child broke into a heavenly smile. Then the scene dissolved and I awoke.

We are told that each individual is born again through the resurrection of Jesus Christ from the dead. I, an individual, have found him of whom Moses and the law and the prophets wrote, for when I awoke in that tomb no one else was there. I recognized that tomb to be my skull and when I came out from its base I found the sign of my spiritual birth as a babe wrapped in swaddling clothes, lying on the floor. The word translated "manger" means "floor; the lowest point in the area". So, you see: a child is not born. The child is only a sign of your individual spiritual birth.

It was I who rose in the sepulcher and pushed myself out. It was I who was born anew through the resurrection of Jesus Christ from the dead. After this experience all of my concepts of Jesus Christ crumbled and dissolved, for I knew that the being who was in the beginning with God actually became me that I may become God in the most literal sense. I knew that God was not only crucified upon me, but was buried within me. That I carried in my body the death of Jesus, that his life might be made alive in me.

I was awed at this experience. Knowing all of the things I had done and was still capable of doing, I wondered how I could be the Christ of scripture. Yet I have searched scripture and cannot find any other explanation. I now share with you what I have experienced, for everything recorded there as an event in the life of one called Jesus Christ has unfolded in me.

We are told: "You search the scriptures thinking in them you will find eternal life, yet it is they which bear witness to me." One hundred and thirty-nine days after my resurrection and birth from above my head began to vibrate intensely. Suddenly it burst and I found myself seated in a modestly furnished room. A youth, handsome beyond measure, was leaning against the frame of an open door. As looked at him I knew he was my son, yet I also knew he was David of Biblical fame. At that moment I had found my son and he had found his father.

The next morning as I searched scripture to find out who saw David and whom David called father, this is what I found. In the 89th Psalm, the Lord declared: "I have found David. He has cried unto me, `Thou art my Father, my God and the Rock of my salvation.'"

If David called the Lord his father, and David called me father, am I not the Lord? This is the plan that God established in the beginning when he gave himself to you and to me. Being a father before the pledge, when God succeeds in the giving you and I must be God.

Dwell upon these words: "I am the true and living way to the Father. No one comes unto the Father save by me." This true and living way is a pattern buried in all which leads the individual to the discovery of being God the Father. This truth is revealed by David, for it is he who says: "I will tell of the decree of the Lord. He said unto me, 'Thou art my son, today I have begotten thee.'"

Now, Christ, being God's creative power and wisdom, cannot be separated from God. Christ was not some little boy who was born two thousand years ago, but God's semen, his creative power that is buried in humanity. The image of God is contained within that semen; and if God is a father, when the semen awakens in the individual he will know himself to be God, the father of all life.

One hundred and twenty-three days after the revelation of being God the Father, I fulfilled the 3rd chapter of John, wherein Nicodemus was told: "As Moses lifted up the serpent in the wilderness, so must the Son of man be lifted up." (That which is recorded in the Book of Numbers is an adumbration of the event, for when the Son of man is lifted up it is an extremely personal experience.)

That night a bolt of lightning split my body from the top of my head to the base of my spine, becoming a pool of golden liquid light. Knowing it was myself, I knew I was self-redeemed. I fused with the light and becoming one with it I ascended my spine to enter my skull, where the drama began. As I did my skull reverberated from the intensity of the vibration, and once again scripture was fulfilled.

There is no other purpose in life other than to fulfill scripture. You may own all of Caesar's belongings, but when you depart this world you must leave it all behind. But when God's pattern erupts in you, you enter an eternal world, knowing yourself to be its creative power. Then you are used to express God in any aspect your very being so desires.

The fourth and final revelation occurs 998 days later. This event brings the total number of days from the birth from above to the discovery of the dove to 1210 – as foretold in the books of Daniel and Revelation. On this final day my skull became transparent, as a lovely beige dove floated about twenty feet above me. As I raised my right hand the dove descended and lit upon my index finger. Then I brought it to my face and it smothered me with affection.

Here again scripture was fulfilled as the Holy Spirit descended upon me in bodily form as a dove, revealing the story of Jesus Christ as a personal experience. When I was physically born, it was through the action of powers not my own and I had no consciousness of it. But my spiritual birth was consciously experienced from beginning to end.

This is my story. It is my hope that you will follow me. That you will believe my experiences. If I tell you earthly things and you do not believe me, how can I expect you to believe the heavenly things I share with you?

Everyone imagines! Can you believe that Christ, Imagination's power, is in you? If so, then God is in you! And if God is in you, you cannot be lost for then God would be lost. Everyone has to be redeemed. Everyone will be saved because God – the savior of each individual – is redeeming himself, bringing the individual awareness in whom He is buried back into the kingdom with him.

The moment God buried himself in you he imprinted himself upon you, predestining you to not only radiate and reflect God's glory, but to be the express image of his person. God is not some impersonal force, but a person. The unknown author of the letters to the Hebrews claimed he was the express image of God's person. This is a true statement. Not one will be lost because all of us will be gathered together into that one body, one Spirit, one Lord, one God and Father of all. In the end there will be one grand fulfillment of the greatest of all commandments: "Hear, O Israel, the Lord our God, the Lord is one."

When I speak of my imagination there appears to be two of us: Neville, and my imagination. I know imagination cannot be seen, yet I also know I cannot separate myself from it. If I lose myself in a daydream and move from my living room in Beverly Hills to Central Park in New York City, I have not separated myself from my creative power. I cannot, for my imagination is my very being. I can speak of my imagination, but I cannot separate myself from it any more than God can be separated from Divine Imagination, for through Divine Imagination's creativity God creates and sustains the world. Should God change his imagining the world would cease to exist, because it must be, and is supported by an imaginal act. The same thing is true in your world. It will change only when you cease to continue to dwell in your current imaginal state!

But there is a pattern buried in you that will not change. Told in the form of a story, man thinks an individual was born two thousand years ago. But the creative power of God did not assume only one man; he took human nature into his sacred Self. The one creative power of the universe is buried in humanity. It is the same creative power in one who murders, as in the one who is murdered. God allows you to misuse Christ, his creative power. But in the end, He will awaken and all violence within you will cease to be, for you will discover yourself to be infinite love, infinite wisdom, and infinite power. Then the world will become a shadow, and you will know there is no need to fight shadows.

Now let me share two experiences of one who knows herself to be an incurrent eyewitness. She has the capacity to turn her thoughts inward and see a world as solid and real as our outer one appears to be.

This particular day she decided to leave the scene that was before her eyes by turning inward and claiming it had vanished. But instead of vanishing, the scene froze and everything became a cold, dead statue. Realizing that she had the power to arrest it, she decided to test herself to see if she could re-animate the scene once more. So, she imagined the scene was alive and instantly life flowed through the room, as though no action on her part had ever stopped its flow. Then she said to herself: "If I can stop and start what the world calls vision, I should be able to stop and start what the world calls reality." She can, for in that brief vision she learned where life really is. Christ in her gave her a taste of the power she will exercise consciously in the not distant future.

Although this world appears so very real, it is a vision. "All that you behold, though it appears without, it is within, in your Imagination of which this world of mortality is but a shadow." If life is in God and God is your imagination, then what the world calls life is only an activity of your imagination. If you stop imagining and arrest that which seems to be animated and independent of your perception, you will prove to yourself that it can be done. Then you will know who Christ is, for you will have discovered that "In him is life and his life is the light of men." God animates Man within himself. Although humanity appears to be independent, with life in themselves, their life is but an activity of imagination, for that is what I AM!

My friend also shared this experience. One night in dream she was in a classroom listening to a woman teach the law. Claiming to believe and practice the law, the woman began to rant and rave against Neville, claiming he was insane, as she did not believe in the promise. The lady then asked the teacher: "Do you believe that imagining creates reality?" and when the woman replied, Yes, the lady asked: "How would you feel right now if you began to imagine you were God?" With that the teacher screamed: ""You should be in the same institution with Neville!""

It is easy to mouth the words: imagining creates reality, but are you willing to imagine you are God? And if you did would you become God? At that thought a line was drawn, so she does not really believe that imagining creates reality. She is willing to believe that she can imagine things are better than they seem to be, but to believe she is God is an insane thought.

Her dream fulfilled the 10th chapter of John, where the question is asked: "Why listen to him? The man is mad and has a demon." When one comes to tell the story of God becoming Man that Man may become God, he is called mad, because his words are in conflict with what the world believes.

This is always true. If anyone told our forefathers that electricity was a fact – that by merely turning a switch a room would be ablaze with light, he would have been called crazy and condemned. In certain sections of time, if a thought was in conflict with what the churches taught, one could be burned at the stake.

Every man who awakens to his infinite power is considered mad. His words are considered those of the devil, for his experiences do not conform to what men think Christ is. Men are looking for some super being to come out of the clouds and save the people who are now dead, and treat the others horribly. But if someone comes and claims that there is only one savior and that one is in everyone as his awareness, that one is considered mad and possessed by the devil.

But I tell you: God acts the moment you imagine. You are the temple of the living God and the spirit of God dwells in you. In the 10th chapter of Hebrews this temple is identified with the curtain which, when torn from top to bottom, opens up the new and living way. Then, ascending in consciousness, you take your own blood into the presence of the Living God.

Paul asks the question: "Do you not know you are the temple of the living God and the spirit of God dwells in you?"[1] If the curtain of that temple is torn from top to bottom, it has to be you! The spirit who ascends is he who is buried in you, and will rise in the same manner as Moses lifted up the serpent in the wilderness. So, when I ask you to follow me, I mean it literally, for I am telling you what I know from experience. I am not theorizing or speculating. Redemption is a very personal experience that takes place in the individual you.

No one really dies, for the world does not cease to exist when your senses cease to register it. Your friends and loved ones who have departed this world are just as real to themselves as when they were here. Now clothed in bodies like yours and mine, they are in a terrestrial world fulfilling their unfulfilled desires. While there they will know the same struggles, joy and sorrow, peace and war, as Christ continues to awaken God's image in them.

When God said: "Let us make man in our image," He placed that image in you. And when Christ is born in you, you – the express image of the invisible God – enter the kingdom, radiating and reflecting God's glory.

There are those who believe they are reborn by changing their attitude and giving more money to the church. That is because they do not know the mystery of Christ. My visions would frighten them and they would call me mad; yet I am telling the truth which I know from experience. I am not trying to share some workable philosophy of life.

Another lady wrote telling of a dream in which she found herself standing in a long line, moving towards a man sitting behind a desk. When she arrived, he stamped the back of her left hand with indelible ink and she intuitively knew this was her

---

[1] *1 Cor. 3:16*

entrance into heaven. A few nights later she found herself on a highway protected by chains. Seeing two secondary roads leading off the highway, she knew she had formerly walked there, but was now on the road towards the kingdom of heaven.

These dreams are foreshadowings – healthy experiences to encourage her to persist. She has now found the one and only way to the Father. That way is I am! Believing in the Father, she will find him, and when she does she will find her very self!

We are told that God speaks to man through the medium of dream and makes himself known in vision. If this is true, no voice should interest you more than that which is heard in your dreams and visions. Words spoken by men of the world are spoken from theory. They voice their opinions, but I am telling you my revelations.

This night I have told you how Christ is formed. As Paul said: "My little children with whom I am again in labor until Christ be formed in you." Just like a child is being formed in the womb of a woman, when Christ is formed in you it comes forth. Then you awaken to discover you have been sound asleep throughout the centuries, although you did not know it.

The world, seeing a mortal body cremated and turned to dust, cannot understand how there can be a head that survives such an experience; but it does, for the real Man is all Imagination. He imagines a body there just as easily as he imagines one here. When you see a friend or dear one who has departed you will recognize him, but he will be young, as he is continuing the work that he set out to do, which is to form Christ in him.

One of the signs of your spiritual birth will be the three witnesses. As I stood watching them their thoughts were objective to me. I was unseen by them because spirit was born. As spirit, I was invisible to my mortal brothers who came to witness the event.

Unless one is born into the spirit world, when he leaves this world of flesh and blood he is not spirit but solidly real, as we are here. He is not seen by mortal eye because a veil has been drawn.

But after your spirit is born the veil is removed from your spiritual eyes, and you will realize humanity is doing what must be done in order for God's image to be formed in them.

Every man's words are his judge. Believe me and follow me into an entirely different sphere known as the kingdom of God.

Now let us go into the silence.

Feel Deeply

What you feel deeply is far more important than what you are thinking. You may think about doing something for a long time and never do it, but when you feel something deeply you are spurred to act – and God acts! He who is the cause of all life acts through the sense of feeling. You can think of a thousand things, yet not be moved to act upon one of them. A deep conviction – felt, is far more important than anything you could ever think.

Let us turn to the first chapter of the epistle of James. "Ask in faith with no doubting, for he who doubts is like the wave of the sea that is driven and tossed by the wind. Let not that person believe that a double-minded man, unstable in all his ways, shall receive anything from the Lord. But be ye doers of the word and not hearers only, deceiving yourself. For if you are a hearer only and not a doer, you are like a man who observes his natural face in the mirror and then goes his way, forgetting what he is like. But if you are a doer of the word and not just a forgetful hearer, you will look into the perfect law of liberty, and persevere. That man shall be blessed in all his doings."

How do you go about being a doer in place of a hearer only? By acting in faith. Scripture's central character, called Jesus, set no limit upon the love of God and the power of faith. In fact, all of his great deeds were prefaced with the words: "According to your faith." Now, faith encompasses feeling. If you have faith you will act, and if you act God in you is acting, for God is your own wonderful human imagination whose eternal name is I AM. He acts only when you feel it. This is true even in the most practical way.

If I tell you what I would like to be and you tell me to go my way, as I am already it – and for one fleeting moment I see the world as I would see it if it were true, then turn and walk away, forgetting what the world looked like only a moment before – I am a forgetful hearer. But if I am a doer of the word and not a hearer only, I persevere; or – as the word is translated in the King James Version – I "continue in" the state, for all things are possible to the power of the word.

Look in a mirror and you will see your face reflected there, but you have another mirror which you can look into. That is the mirror of your friends; if they heard your good news, their faces would reflect it would they not? Assume your desire is now a fact. Feel its substance and reality. Then let your friends see you in that state. They are your living mirror.

Now persevere in that state and do not turn away and quickly forget what you are like. Walk through this door tonight in the assumption that you are the man (or woman) you want to be. It doesn't make any difference if the outside denies it; you have seen the expression on the faces of your friends and heard their congratulations on the inside, with faith. Now, carry this feeling into the deep and persevere. Conjure a living mirror of friends and acquaintances who have heard your good news and accepted it as permanent. See your face reflected in theirs. If they love you, you will see empathy. They will be rejoicing because of your good fortune. Now, persevere in that awareness and do not forget what you have seen in your living mirror. If you do, you will be blessed in the doing, as you are told in the first chapter of the Book of Psalms: "Blessed is the man who delights in the law of the Lord; the perfect law of liberty, for in all that he does, he prospers."

Were you not liberated from your past when you saw your friend's faces reflecting what you wanted them to see? If you had left the state of poverty, sickness, or weakness behind and moved into the state of wealth, health, or strength – and your friends knew it – you would be set free from your former limitation. So, looking into the perfect law of liberty and persevering, you are blessed in all that you do.

I tell you from personal experience that this works, but we are the operant power. It does not operate itself. You may have heard this law by the hearing of the ear and read of it in a book, but do you know that the law works from experience? Have you put it to the test? Have you proved it? If you have, then you can speak with an authority, which was not yours prior to the proving. May I tell you: through the use of this law you are completely set free.

I have been in many places where I was forced to test this principle. While on the little island of Barbados, which had only two small ships servicing it as well as the hundreds of islands nearby, I made a commitment to give a series of lectures in Milwaukee on the first of May. When I called, the shipping agent informed me that due to the fact that the ship sailing out of New York City carried only sixty passengers and the one from Boston carried only one hundred, that there was no passage available before the first of September. He promised to put my name on the waiting list, but gave me no encouragement as the list was very long.

I hung up the phone and sat in my chair in the hotel room, closed my eyes and assumed I was aboard a ship heading toward New York City. I assumed eight or ten of my family were coming aboard with me, and that my brother Victor was carrying my little girl. I could feel the motion of the plank. Having no stateroom committed, I remained on deck and placed my mental hands on the rail and felt the salt of the sea there. Then I looked back nostalgically at the little island. I repeated that action over and over again, feeling every step I made on that gangplank. I felt the rail and smelled the salt of the sea. I did everything that feeling could be brought to bear upon, and when my actions seemed natural, I broke it.

The very next day I received confirmation that I would be sailing on a ship which would land in New York City one week before my commitment in Milwaukee, which I did. When I asked the agent how I obtained the tickets, he said they had a cancellation in New York and the one person he had called on the waiting list felt that the timing was inconvenient; so – knowing he could accommodate my wife, our little daughter and myself in one cabin – he let us in. I never heard why someone canceled in New York or why the one he called in Barbados could not take the ship at that time, or why the agent did not call all the others on the waiting list. I only know that I got the reservation I had imagined.

I have told this story before, and someone in the audience once said; "Was that a Christian thing to do? You might have caused someone to cancel their trip." But I tell you, as I told her: it was the only Christian thing to do, for I used the Christian principle of fulfilling God's law. How it is going to be fulfilled is not my concern. I am told that whatever I desire, if I will but believe I have received it, I will. God never creates a desire in the human heart that he has not already provided its satisfaction. This is true of every desire in this world, as well as the greatest of all desires, which is the thirst for God.

Do you really want an experience of God? Apply this principle towards it. Do what I did when I wanted to leave Barbados and come to America. I looked into the perfect law of liberty and persevered. God doesn't give you one law for your desires of this world and another law for your search for him. It's the same law. If you have had the experience of which I speak, would you tell someone about it? Is it a consuming desire, or do you want something other than that first? Perhaps you want a lovely home, security in the sense of money in the bank that you can touch, or stocks and bonds that pay dividends. If you want to feel wealthy, travel, and have lots of things before you thirst for an experience of Christ, it is secondary, so don't try it. But if an experience of Christ is your consuming desire then don't hesitate to put it to the test. Put first things first. If your first desire is to be recognized in the work that I am doing, then apply this principle towards it and let that thirst for God take its own good time to envelop you, and when it does apply this principle towards it.

Feel in depth, for what you feel deeply is more vital than what you think. Every day you can think about how wonderful it would be if – and never act. But if every day you would feel how wonderful it is now, it will become true. Shakespeare said: "Assume a virtue if you have it not." A virtue must be felt to be assumed. Refrain from the assumption tonight and it will be easy to refrain next week and still easier the next. But if you will assume your desire is fulfilled now, and persevere in that assumption through the sense of feeling, it will be externalized as a literal fact in your world.

I am calling upon everyone to put this into practice. Every desire contains its own satisfaction to be fed upon. It's entirely up to you. You may feed your hunger by thinking of your desire, or feed its satisfaction by thinking from its fulfillment. It is God who gives you every desire, be it for things of this age or the age to come – as told us in the Book of Amos: "I will send a famine upon the world. It will not be a hunger for bread or a thirst for water, but for the hearing of the word of God."

When you want to speak the word of God, your hunger is not for the hearing of the word, but for the glamour connected with the teaching. It is the spotlight you desire and that too has been provided for. Every desire can and will be satisfied if you will look into the law of liberty and persevere. Then you will be blessed in all you do.

A chap came to see me from New York City yesterday. When I heard his request, I would not tell him my reaction to it, but that I would hear that he had it. This chap, now retired from the antique department of Macy's, has been teaching in one of these isms back East. Then he started corresponding with a group out here, who – unable to believe in themselves – wants a leader; so they have asked him to come lead them. When he told me the nature of his desire I was sorry that all he could see in life was the spotlight, but I granted it to him. He is tired of playing third, fourth or fifth fiddle to a leader who has milked a million dollars out of those who are buying bricks into heaven. Having nothing, this man's followers are building heaven for him and giving it to him as their gift. They have bought valuable land in New York City and built a building on it. Then he threw a banquet at a large hotel and they paid $50 for the privilege of seeing the mortgage they paid for burned, but the land and building are in his name.

Back in 1943, this same man told me he was coming to New York for only one purpose and that was to make money in the so-called New Thought movement. When I heard him say this, I thought he was in the wrong profession. If he wanted to make a lot of money he should go into steel, oil, or coal. If you want to do this work you can live well, but will not have the ambition for millions. Well, he wanted lots of money and now he has it, as well as homes in the country, an apartment in the city, and a lovely, large building in New York City – which those who love to be milked paid for. The chap who came to see me assisted this man. He has seen how phony it has been, but he hasn't completely overcome it. He still wants the spotlight and now he has the opportunity to get it. I will pray for his success – not as a teacher for he is not one – but for the glamour he will receive by those who want the nonsense, as they are going to start off by not eating meat, smoking, or drinking – in fact a complete loss of the palate.

His request does not offend my moral code, so I can easily say that he is successful; but I urge you who are sincere to try to create within yourself a longing for the deepest of all desires, and that is to know God from experience. If you can really thirst for God above everything else, then use the same law of liberty. Look into the faces of your friends and say with deep conviction and feeling: "I have had the experiences of which Neville speaks. The entire series, from the resurrection through the descent of the dove, has unfolded within me." Then persevere, for God has provided a satisfaction for that hunger and you will know it. But if this hunger is not yet upon you and you sincerely want a better way of living that is not wrong, simply use the same principle of the perfect law of liberty and persevere. Having acted, don't turn and forget what you have done but sleep in that conviction, and in a way, you do not know, it will be yours.

Tonight, many of our friends are not here because it is Memorial Day. But I tell you: not one moment in time is holier than another and there is no earthly place more sacred than the other. Wherever you stand is sacred ground because you are there. Today millions are celebrating Memorial Day, remembering the dead and placing flowers on a grave their loved ones do not occupy. This morning just prior to waking, I saw my brother Lawrence. He died at the age of sixty-two, but looked much older because he had suffered so much before his departure. This morning he was only about twenty-three years of age. We were both fully awake and he asked me to tell his wife that the money he left her was for her, and not to save it for the children. I said: "Lawrence, you don't have to go through me to tell Doris, she wouldn't give one penny to anyone anyway. She never has. Do you think she would change now? Her only concern is that you did not give it all to her, but shared equally with your four children." But I was with Lawrence. He was strong, strapping and handsome, blond with brown eyes. He is the same Lawrence, with the same intelligence he had when he left here. He is younger now, but he still has the memory of the family he left behind. The veil is no clearer to him there than it is to those on this side. Only one who is awake can penetrate the veil consciously. It is easy now for me to go beyond the world of dream and enter the world of spirit waking and meet my friends there.

But on Memorial Day men think of the dead, while I am speaking of life everlasting. "Let the dead bury the dead," and follow me, for I have risen from the dead and I speak of a Living God who is real. I cannot go to a cemetery and put flowers or a flag on that which is not there. The body may have been placed there, but not the spirit.

You are buried in the skull and in that skull you will remain, dreaming your dream of life until you awaken and are born the second time. It is from there you are going to find David, who reveals you as God the Father. It is from there you are going to be split in two and ascend into the Holy of Holies. You were begotten in that skull and you will end the drama there, to know you are one with the one and only Living God.

In the 25th and 27th chapters of the Book of Genesis, the story is told of Isaac, who had two sons. The first son, Esau, had hair all over while the second son, Jacob, was hairless. Being blind, Isaac calls Esau and asks him to go get some venison for dinner. Jacob, having overheard the request, clothed himself in the skins of his brother Esau and took the venison to his father. Isaac, hearing Jacob's voice began to doubt, until he felt his reality and caught his odor. Satisfying himself that the son was real, Jacob was given the father's blessing. When Esau returned from the hunt Jacob disappeared, but Isaac said: "Although your brother came through deception, I have given him your blessing and I cannot take it back."

After smothering yourself in feeling, you have sent it on its way and cannot take it back, for prayer is nothing more than the subjective appropriation of an objective hope. Imagine by giving objective reality to your hope. Hair is the most objective thing on a man. Bring your hope so close that you can feel what it would be like if it were objective to you.

Clothe yourself in that feeling – and you have clothed yourself in the reality of an Esau. The world will not immediately reflect your feeling, but you have set your desire in motion and cannot take it back. You have given a subjective state your blessing by giving it objective reality. Now it must fulfill its destiny so that you will be blessed in all that you are doing.

If you don't give your subjective hope objective reality, you can't be blessed in its fulfillment. You must clothe yourself in the feeling that your wish is fulfilled. Jacob is your desire, waiting to be clothed in the feeling of external reality. Catch the feeling, and you have clothed Jacob with the external reality of Esau. Now deceive yourself into believing that your desire is externally real and give it your blessing by subjectively appropriating your objective hope. Who is the blind Isaac? You are, for you cannot see what you are asking for in your outer world. It's a hope and you are blind to it. But when you clothe yourself in the feeling of its fulfillment, you are eating the feeling of satisfaction. Feast upon this feeling morning, noon, and night, and in a way, you do not know your desire will become an objective reality in your world.

In this story we see the importance of feeling. Isaac asked Jacob to come close and kiss him. The word translated "kiss" means, "to set on fire; to burn; to touch." That's an emotion, an intense feeling. Reality is felt through the sense of touch. Feeling is touch. Tasting is touch. Scripture tells us he tasted death for all of us. How do you taste death? By experiencing it. Jesus tasted death by dying in all, that all may know who he is.

Now I urge you to put his teaching into practice. He taught you to simply appropriate a subjective state which is your objective hope, and know it must externalize itself in your world. Do that and it will. Ask in faith, without a doubt, for those who doubt are like the wave of the sea that is driven and tossed by the wind. They are double-minded, for they know what they are while desiring to be something else. You must be single-minded by dropping what you believe you are and assuming that you are already what you desire to be, for you cannot desire something you already possess. Look into the wonderful law of liberty which sets you free, and you will see your freedom in the faces of your friends. Persist in your assumption and it must come to pass.

Now let us go into the silence.

Faith, Hope *and* Love

Scripture makes the most profound statements in the world. You can believe them or reject them, but you will never know their truth until scripture is experienced. When it is once experienced, you can no more deny it than you can the humblest evidence of your senses.

I make the claim God is love. Scripture tells us God is faith, saying: "Through faith the world was made by the Word of God." And we are told to "Put your hope fully upon the grace that is coming to you at the resurrection of Jesus Christ in you." Now, I can tell you that his name is I AM and that God's first revelation to man is that of the Father. I can tell you that all this is true of yourself; that you are God the Father; that you are infinite love, infinite faith, and infinite hope, but you will not know this truth until it becomes your own experience.

After you have experienced scripture, there is no power in the world that can persuade you that you were hallucinating, for when you experience this truth you are on a far greater level of awareness than anything known to man on this level. Whether he be an Einstein, a great financial giant, or a famous doctor, he is aware only of this level and what I speak of here is on an entirely different sphere. What you experience is separate from this world, and that experience is what I call "religion". Religion is a devotion to the reality of an exalted experience, the reality of which reason and the senses may deny, but you will know you had the experience.

Now let me share with you three letters I received this week. One lady – who is very much a lady – writes, "On the night of January 24th I was sitting quietly, meditating, when suddenly something turned or opened in my head and I heard a voice say: 'I am faith, hope and love.' A moment later a deep, gloriously masculine voice added: 'I am the Father.' Those words touched me with such emotion that I burst into tears and cried and cried."

The shortest sentence in scripture is "Jesus wept". At the very end of the drama, one who was supposed to be the rock on which the whole would be established denied the story three times before the cock crowed. Then, remembering all that was foretold, he wept bitterly. Now, to embrace an experience one must have an experiencing nature, for it is only from an experiencing nature that the furnaces of affliction can refine the essence of faith, hope and love.

Here is a statement from the 48th chapter of Isaiah: "Now you will know; now you will hear things that you have never known before. From of old your ears have not been opened, but I tried you in the furnace of affliction. For my own sake, for my own sake I do it, for how can my name be profaned. My glory I will not give to another."

You may think that because you have perfect pitch and can hear the slightest sound that your ears are opened, but they are sealed to the heavenly voices, completely sealed to the heavenly world. But now I tell you: God is love, he is faith, and he is hope. His initial hope was "Let us make man in our image." Having the faith that it could be done, it took love to do it. It is love who is put through the furnace of affliction and – although it seems to be hell while experienced – love turns Man into a living soul so Man can respond, for without response there is no action.

In the silence this lady heard the words: "I am faith, hope and love" followed by a deep, masculine voice saying: "I am the Father". Now she knows that she incarnates God and that he radiates from her own wonderful human imagination. Having had this experience, there is no priest, no minister or archbishop who could persuade her out of it. This lady is unknown to the world, yet she has experienced that which is unknown to its intellectual and financial giants.

I tell you scripture is true, and the day will come when the voice will reveal her as the Father. That is when God's only begotten Son stands before her and calls her "Father." Then she will know and say: "I have found David; he has called me My Father, My God, and the Rock of my salvation."

You might think that a lady could not have the experience of being the Father, but in this dimension of which I speak we are the Elohim. We are not male or female, but God, yet God made up of many. The word "Elohim" is a compound unity, one made up of many. We are all the one Father of the one and only begotten Son, the quintessence of man's experiences, personified as David. The voice who spoke to her declared eternal truth, and when you stand in the presence of the Risen Christ and hear the words, "God is love," you will know its eternal truth. And when he incorporates you into his body, you will not be two anymore, but one. Then, as he incorporates himself into another and still another, we will all be gathered back into the one body, the one Spirit, and we will all know we are the Father. There aren't numberless Fathers. We all fell from the one Father, and we are all gathered together back into the one Father, who said to the lady: "I am the Father." I can't tell you my thrill when I received that letter.

Now, to have a great experience you must have an experiencing nature, for only by an experiencing nature can you devise the essence of faith, hope and love. And when it happens the tears fall. Peter was not emotionally moved when the truth was intellectually heard, but when it was experienced and the whole thing came to pass in him, he wept bitterly. One day you will experience scripture and know how true it is. I am speaking from experience when I tell you that I stood in the presence of the Risen Christ and spoke the words of Paul: "Faith, hope and love, these three, but the greatest of these is love." Then I was embraced by Man who is infinite love, who is God. And what I have experienced you will experience also.

There are those who speak of God as an over-soul, or impersonal force. They have become so abstract in their concept of this creative and redeeming power. But God is not an over-soul or intangible force, but Man, and he speaks with a voice as I speak to you now. You hear me in the tongue in which you were born. When God speaks to you, you will hear him in your natural tongue. And when you stand in the presence of Infinite love it is Man, and yet you will know he is all love.

Now let me share another experience. We are told in the Book of Genesis that when a dream is doubled, God has fixed it and it will shortly come to pass. This lady had three dreams of elephants. In her first dream she said: "It was the mating season, and I saw many elephants, all in the creative act." This dream was followed by a dream in which she found herself standing by a river, surrounded by mountains. On the river's bank stood three stone elephants, and as she looked at them they became animated, entered the river, and swam downstream. Watching them she said to herself: "This is the second time I have seen stone elephants. The last time was when they came out of the mountains." Then she added: "When I awoke I realized what I had said was true."

There is a language of symbolism that is universal. Regardless of whether you are in Africa, in China or here, in the depth of the soul the elephant is the symbol of God's creative power and wisdom, which is defined in scripture as Jesus Christ. In her dream she remembered another dream, so this dream is bordering on self-revelation, which is God revealing himself in her.

God's creative power has made itself known to her and she will, in the immediate present, have tangible proof of the fact that her own wonderful human imagination is Christ Jesus. All things are possible to God, and by the exercise of this power she can prove that she is the creative power of the universe. Symbolized as in the creative act, this power appeared as stone which has not been made alive. Something was seemingly dead in her world, but it doesn't matter, the power is not there. It's not in space, in the stars, or teacup leaves. Power is not in anything outside of the human imagination. All that you behold, though it appears without, it is within, in your imagination of which this world of mortality is but a shadow. To prove this to herself, she saw the elephants as dead, all made of stone. Is there anything more inanimate, more dead, than stone? Yet the moment she beheld them they became animated and entered the stream of life.

She was in a wonderful mountainous area, and all through scripture revelations took place from the mountaintops. Jesus was on the mountaintop when he transfigured himself, and now, here in this mountainous area, her own creative power was revealed. So, I repeat: God the creator and your own wonderful human imagination are one and inseparable; therefore, he will never be so far off as even to be near, for nearness implies separation. Now she knows – as does the other lady – that she incarnates God, and God radiates from her as her own wonderful human imagination.

What are you imagining right now? Is it something disastrous? Or is it a wonderful thought that has caught fire within you? No matter what your thoughts may be, they will come to pass, for there is nothing in this world but that which was first imagined. In the January issue of a magazine called The National Observer, there is a picture of a demolished railroad threshold. You see a large section of the train broken, with many cars demolished and one suspended over the edge of an embankment. It is a photograph of an accident which happened recently in Rubin, Idaho. This same picture had appeared in their December issue, and when a reader in Springfield, Virginia saw it, he thought it strangely familiar. Then he remembered that nineteen years ago he had been sketching, and a scene just came out of his imagination, a scene that was a duplicate of the accident that happened this past year. Sending a picture of his sketch to The National Observer, he asked: "Is it fate that my picture so closely resembles the actual accident?" He thought the train wreck was the actual event, but it was the effect. He was the cause. This is a world of shadows. He drew the accident, even to the trees surrounding it, and what he called the actual event was only the effect in the shadow world.

So, I say to this lady: you have touched the depth of your soul, the creative power of God, and no one is going to take it from you, for your power has grown to the point of revelation. You can't turn back now and believe in any outside God. Those who have not had the vision can still turn back. They are those on whom the seed fell, and although they eagerly took it, the cares of the world took them away. Or those that, because the seed fell among thorns, it was cast off. Or those that, traveling the highway of life, they tried and proved their creative power but decided that it would have happened anyway, or that it was just coincidence. But in your case, my dear, you can't turn back. There is no power on earth that can turn you back to any orthodox belief, for you have seen the symbol of the creative power of God. Starting as the creative act, you turned stone into something alive and it has entered the stream of life. You know now that you have the power to take something that is dead and barren as stone and in your mind's eye resurrect it, breathe upon it, and make it alive.

Now, the other letter was from a gentleman. His is on another level. In his dream he sees a house from which a glow radiates from its windows and doors. Someone near asked: "When you enter the house, how will we know you are doing it?" And he answered: "I only do what is necessary, but no matter what I do you will still say it is a trick." Then a voice spoke from within him saying: "I have power I know not of." This gentleman has the power to create, but he has not entered the state of consciousness to exercise it. He knows that when he enters this house and things happen, it is he who says it would have happened anyway. There are no others, there is only God in this world. Although he answered the question, there was doubt, and he always takes it with him as he enters a new state of consciousness, therefore never quite sure that his imaginal act was the cause of the phenomena of his life.

Here we see various levels of the revelation of God within Man. The first one was the fantastic "I am the Father" and in the not distant future she will know this truth in the most intimate manner. No longer will it be as a voice coming from the depth of her soul, but she will know she is the Father when God's only begotten Son stands before her and calls her "Father." In the meantime, God is radiating from her own wonderful human imagination. She knows that I am Faith, I am Hope and I am Love. She has read it in the 13th chapter of Corinthians. She has heard it from the platform, but she knows it now from revelation. She heard the words coming from within herself and when David, in the Spirit, calls her Lord, she will prove to herself that everything I say from the platform is true.

So I repeat: We will not know scriptural truth until it is experienced, and then we cannot deny it any more than we can the humblest evidence of our senses. God's first revelation to Man is Power, Almighty God, El Shaddai. His second revelation is I AM. "My name is in you, listen, take heed, harken to my voice, for my name is in you." And his final revelation is that of Father.

In the 40th Psalm it is said: "Thou hast given me an open ear." This is repeated in the 10th chapter of Hebrews in this manner: "Sacrifices and offerings thou hast not desired, but a body thou hast prepared for me." The open ear of Psalms has now become a body, an immortal body that cannot die. Something turned and opened, and although from of old the lady had not heard, now she hears. Your garment of flesh and blood has ears, but I speak of an entirely different body. I speak of the body which has been put through the furnaces, which has been prepared for the heavenly kingdom. So, judge not from appearances, for although they may be famous and extremely rich they are still asleep, and when they depart this world they will enter another world of the dead. But she – although unknown here – will enter the world of life, for her body has been prepared for the age that is to come.

Your faith is justified not by any argument, but by an experience. Tell me what you believe and I will hear your confession of faith. Tonight, believe the words the lady heard. Say within yourself: "I am the Father" and you will hear your own confession of faith. That is where the true spirit of scripture is – all within self. And God's creative power is in you. So if tonight you want something, know it is contained within you and you have the power to animate it and make it alive. Then have faith, have confidence that in its own good time what you have imagined will come to pass. You need not tell anyone or devise the means of its fulfillment. All you need is faith. Through faith we understand that the world was created by the Word of God. So set your hope fully upon this grace of God which is the hope of Man. God gave himself to you as though there were no other, and when his Son stands before you and calls you "Father" you will know that faith has transformed itself into vision, that hope has been completely realized, and that love endureth forever.

Now let us go in to the silence.

Freedom

When asked: "What is the greatest of all the commandments?" God answered: "Hear O Israel, the Lord our God, the Lord is one." Accept this commandment! Live by it and you will be free from all secondary causes. There is only one God. He is the father of us all who is above all, through all, and in all. He is a universally diffused individuality whose name forever and ever is I AM. You may not be aware of who you are, what you are, or where you are; but by being aware, you are mentally saying I am. Every conscious being says I am; and if there is only one I am, then I am one individual – diffused! I am the sole cause of all that is. All things were made through imagining, and without awareness was not anything made that was made.

In the 8th chapter of Matthew, one of the miracles of scripture is recorded as an acted parable. It is said that when he entered the boat, he fell asleep and a great storm arose; so they woke him saying: "Lord we perish, save us." And he said: "Why are you afraid, O men of little faith?" Then he rose and rebuked the wind and the sea, and there was a great calm. If there is only one cause, then he who quelled the wind and the sea is the one who caused the storm. There cannot be another. If there is confusion in your life, and you resolve it in your imagination, and the world bears witness to what you have done – you caused the change. And since there is no other cause, then did you not cause the confusion also? There is only one God and Father of us all who is above all, through all, and in all. If He is in every being who says I am, and there is only one God, no one can accuse another; for God's name is not he is, but I am. No matter what appears on the outside, I am its cause. Assume full responsibility for the things you observe, and if you do not like what you see, know you have the power to change them. Then exercise that power and you will observe the change you caused. If you are truly willing to assume that responsibility, you are set free.

If this universal diffused individuality is in all, then the incarnation must be regarded in a different light. We were taught that the incarnation took place 2000 years ago by a unique individual, who was the incarnate God. But I tell you: humanity is the incarnation. The central figure – personified as Jesus Christ – is the perfect archetypal figure everyone must express. He is called the true witness, the first-born of the dead. Now incarnate in your body of flesh and blood, you are dead in the sense that you have forgotten that you are the creator of all things, and do not see yourself creating anything you observe. The morning paper tells of what she, he, and they, are doing, and you cannot relate their actions to anything you have done; yet there is only one cause, only one God, who is resident in you as your awareness, your own wonderful human imagination.

The parable tells us that God entered a boat and fell asleep. Humanity is that boat, the ark where God the Father creates as he slumbers. Even though you do not know the people you read about, if the reading disturbs you, you are the cause of that conflict. All imagination, I am dreaming, causing the misfortune and unhappiness of those whose lives I have touched with feeling. When you awaken and recall your dream, do you always know the people there? Do you know the children that were yours in the dream? The people who frightened you? You never saw them before, so how could they be other than that which you caused? You do not recognize them, yet you – the dreamer – caused them to do what they did. The same thing is true here. If the actions of a seeming other cause a motor response in you, even though you do not know him, your awareness is the cause of the storm. But when you awake, memory will return and there will be a wonderful calm.

God, the universally diffused individuality, is asleep in everyone. His transcendent revelation is personified as one called Jesus Christ. Thus, personification awakens the memory in you as to who God the Father really is. God did not break up the I am and give each one of us a portion of himself. He gave each one, individually, his whole being. I am cannot be divided, and I am God the Father. If you haven't yet discovered this, I am still asleep. In order to discover your fatherhood, you must find God's son, foretold to be yours. While asleep in the state of Saul, you do not recognize him; and when you ask: "Whose son are you, young man?" he answers: "I am the son of Jesse, the I am." When you awake and recognize God's son, David, are you not Jesse? Are you not God, whose name forever and ever is I am?

It takes David to reveal you to yourself; yet you were his father before you fell asleep. Now dreaming your life into being, you fight against seeming others, calling them devils and Satan. You endow your shadow world with causation, thereby becoming a divided being, when God is not divided. There is no devil. There is no Satan. There is no being outside of your own wonderful human imagination.

"I, even I am he. I kill and I make alive. I wound and I heal and none can deliver out of my hand."[2] "I am the Lord and there is no other God. I form the light and I create darkness. I make the weal and I create woe. I am the Lord and there is no other; besides me there is no God."[3] He who creates the evil, creates the good, the weal and the woe, the light and the darkness. He who kills is he who makes alive, and he who wounds is he who heals and there is no other God. If you really believe you are the one spoken of here – that it is you who create the evil, the good, the weal and the woe; that none can deliver out of your hand – then you are set free. You will never again believe in another, but know that your life is self-created. That you create the storms, as well as the peace and the calm. No longer will you believe he, she, or they, did it, for you will recognize them as reflections mirroring either the storm or the peace and calm within you.

---

[2] *Deut. 52*
[3] *Isaiah 45*

Having entered the boat (called the ark) God fell asleep and there he remains until the dove brings him word that the flood of illusion is over. Dramatized as an acted parable, it is said that Noah put forth his hand and brought the dove into the ark with him. This is beautiful imagery and true. In my vision the dove descended through what appeared to be crystal clear water. He seemed to float, using his wings like a swan. Lighting upon my extended finger he smothered me with kisses as the vision came to its end.

Because everyone is the whole God, everyone will personify the perfect archetypal specimen called Jesus Christ. Lost in confusion, not knowing that humanity is the incarnation, men think of this archetypal specimen as the incarnate God. Yet the one grand commandment is: "Hear O Israel, the Lord our God, the Lord is one." The word Israel means: the man who rules – not like a god, but as God, because he knows he is God. And the word translated "Lord" is I AM. Now let me translate it for you: Hear, O man who rules as God, the I AM, our I am is one I AM. We are not a bunch of little I am's. Our I am is the one I AM who is God the Father. If this is true, then God cannot be divided; and the whole of him is wherever you are, wherever I am. There is no he, she, or they, in I am!

If you will completely accept this, you will set yourself free. You may not immediately see the effect of what you have done in your imagination; but it must come, because there is no other creator to stop it. All things are made through awareness, and without it is not anything made that is made. It is imagination who claims: "I kill and I make alive, I wound and I heal. I form the light and create darkness. I form the evil and I make the good, the weal and the woe, and there is no other."

When the Jesuits speak of Satan, devils, and demons, it is because they do not know the greatest commandment. All of the Ten Commandments are based upon the negative thou shall not, except one, which is: "Love thy father and mother." The commandment found in the 6th chapter of Deuteronomy, with ten words, contains all Ten Commandments in an entirely different presentation as: "Hear O Israel, the Lord our God, the Lord is one."

Maybe you cannot accept my words now. Perhaps you feel the need to blame another – to have a scapegoat and believe the cause to be something you ate or drank – but why did you do it? What caused you to do exactly what you did? A disturbance in you! The storm in you caused the gland to be out of kilter. The gland cannot be the cause of your distress, but your dream can. The world, not knowing the single cause, will try to find something on the outside; but there is no secondary cause!

I received a letter this week from a lady who shared this self-revealing dream, saying: "I am in a place totally devoid of comfort. There are no curtains at the windows or rugs on the floor. My sons – in clean overalls – are sitting in straight back chairs against one wall, while my daughters – in starched, long cotton dresses – it opposite them. Looking much like the Quaker children here, my children appear to be without emotion, without feeling, or creative abilities. We are waiting for father! A young boy enters with a message stating that the work which had to be done in the children is finished, and therefore the father is not returning. "Then the scene changes and we are in a farm house. I look out the window to see fields of golden grain ripe for harvest. My eldest son, now radiantly happy, comes running into the house exclaiming that, for the first time, he has created for himself. His entrance was like magic, transforming the room, as all of my children began to use their talents – creating, laughing, animated, and alive. Before, like automatons, they had only obeyed the father by executing his will; but now that his work is finished, he has withdrawn himself, and they have become creators in themselves.

What a beautiful experience. She saw the world in miniature form. The father's withdrawal is recorded as his death. He tells us: "Unless I die thou canst not live, but if I die I shall arise again and thou with me. A little while and you will see me no more; again, a little while and you will see me as yourself." Having withdrawn to dwell within, it is from there that you move, and not from without. All that I – the father – am, you will know yourself to be. If God is the father of all life, then you are the father. If he is a creator, you are a creator. Whatever God is, you will know yourself to be.

Now, God comes out of the desert with signs and wonders. The most outstanding sign is that of the fiery serpent, for everyone who sees it, lives. As your journey out of Egypt begins, the fiery serpent is released when the curtain is torn from top to bottom and all of the rocks are split. You are destined to fulfill scripture and, like me, know from personal experience that you are God the Father. I have shared my visions with you, telling you how true and wonderful the story of scripture really is and that there is only one way of salvation. Although unnumbered volumes have been written giving you many ways of redemption, there is only one. I am the way, and there is no other way.

Matthew tells the story of his awakening in dramatic form. Claiming "they" awoke, saying: "Lord, we perish, save us." It is the unearthly wind which awakens you, and you are its cause. Awakening within your boat (your ark) you leave it behind as you enter an entirely different world as God the Father. Having purposely imposed the restriction of death upon yourself, knowing that you had the power and the wisdom to overcome it, you laid yourself down and fell asleep in the ark. And when the time is fulfilled, you awaken within that ark, come out, and witness the symbolism of your birth from above. A few months later you fulfill the 89th Psalm as you find David and your memory returns.

In the Book of Samuel, Saul (the demented king) made a promise to anyone who would bring down the giant opposition to Israel that he would set his father free. (This is done by discovering the father of the son.) So, Saul asks David to identify his father, and David says: "I am the son of Jesse, the I AM." So, the father is set free when David brings down the giant, who – in your sleep of death – opposes you, and your memory returns as to who you really are.

Although I answer to an earthly name and sign my checks with it, I know who I am! I can tell you who I am in the hope that you will believe me; but in truth, I am only addressing myself, for I am in you and you are in me, and we are one. Everyone will have the same experience and in the end we will all return to the one body, one Spirit, one Lord, and one God and Father. We will all return from the victorious march through death as the same God, but expanded beyond our wildest dreams because of this excursion of the mind into a world of death which seemed so final. I cannot promise that, if you accept this one hundred per cent you will not have a headache tomorrow, or that the boss will not fire you. But if you accept this, you will know that your boss had no choice in the matter. You will know that you caused the firing. Maybe your dreams transcended your present limited position in that business, and only by being fired could they be realized.

One day I was fired from J. C. Penney Co. Working for a year and a half, running their elevator and being their errand boy, making $22. a week and paying $5. room rent, I could not understand it when they let me go. But my dreams, my desires, transcended my position there, so they had to do what they did in order for my desires to be realized. Believe me, you are the cause of the phenomena of your life – be it good, bad or indifferent. If, to you the news is distasteful, you are the dreamer of that distasteful storm. But the day will come when you will awake to discover that the storm is over. That there is only one cause, and that is awareness! I know it is easier to give advice and show the other person where he is wrong, than it is to acknowledge that he is only reflecting the wrong in you. It is difficult to accept the concept that the world is bearing witness to your thoughts, but it is true. If you do not like something or someone, do not look at it or them; look within to the one who is causing the image.

There is only one God, one cause of all life. He is not only above all and through all; he is in all. The universally diffused individuality is in each one of us in his fullness. Dwelling in each individual bodily, the father sleeps until the storm is over. Then he awakens and rebukes the storm that he created during his sleep, and there is a great calm. If you will accept this as your philosophy of life, and not turn to the left or the right, but claim you are solely responsible for the phenomena of your life, you will find it much easier to live. But if, at times, life seems too hard to bear, and you find a secondary cause, you have created a devil. Devils and satans are formed from man's unwillingness to assume the responsibility of his life. To see another other than self, is to build a golden image. Asking a priest for forgiveness. Calling him father in spite of being told to call no man on earth father. Seeing him as an authority, man goes whoring after a man-made false image.

So, what is freedom worth to you? If you stop short of the ultimate, you do not really want freedom. If you were enslaved, what do you have that you would not willingly give – in its entirety – to be set free? Do you really believe there is only one God, who is in you in his entirety, and his name is I am? You do, although you have forgotten who you are, where you are, or that you have a son; one day the wind will awaken you during a storm, and as you come out of the ark the storm will abate. Then memory will return, as he who has always been your son stands before you and calls you father, as scripture unfolds within; and then you will know that the eternal story was always there. It was a sealed book until it unfolded from within.

Let the world remain in the storm if they want to, but if you accept my words you will be set free from any secondary cause, and you who have been causing your storm will find peace and be truly set free.

Now let us go into the silence.

🐝

Also Available from This Author

www.ingramcontent.com/pod-product-compliance
Lightning Source LLC
Chambersburg PA
CBHW020443030426
42337CB00014B/1377

* 9 7 8 1 6 0 3 8 6 7 6 8 9 *